# Amoresia

Love Sonnets of
## Bernard Filipow

tellwell

Tellwell Talent
www.tellwell.ca

ISBN
978-0-2288-2593-7 (Hardcover)
978-0-2288-2591-3 (Paperback)
978-0-2288-2592-0 (eBook)

To my dear and brilliant wife, Giudita,
and my loving and inspirational
mother, Roma.

# I

*O*, sweet scented growths ever unfolding
And daring thieves of Hyperion's Light,
Thy fauvist beauty to my love must bring,
In the fullness of day or in lunar's light,
A rainbow's palate her heart to inspire
And open its gate to a loving admirer,
Whose own heart is filled with love and desire
And with passion burns as our star's own fire.
Yet, above all else you must stay sunfast,
Lest the power of your hues will not last
And their message too short will not persist,
Alas, my deep affections she may resist.
But, if in all this you will succeed,
Your life's sacrifice will honour love's deed.

## II

'Twas only as brief as a dove's wing flash,
With thee bathed in the gilded morning sun,
Did I see your lovely face framed in sash
And knew our hearts could be as one.
I did not know what instincts were at play,
Nor did I care to question their intent,
For the joy I felt stole my senses away,
As if you were from Hera's heaven sent.
Now, I hope the fates may soon intervene
And again behold your countenance,
To prove it not a mirage I had seen
And solve this mystery of romance.
Alas, I pray your feelings be the same
And that the love I felt was not in vain.

# III

*U*shering the Horae to come and go
On shifting landscapes of humanity,
Orchestrating the flights of leaves and snow
While the weak struggle for their sanity.
Shouting with a violent, raging tongue
When jousting the enshrouded on the run
And vying to heckle the bleached sun,
As if the contest was already won.
How so the north wind doth fatefully blow
When complying with nature's destiny
And Boreus screams that each might know
His cold mystic force rages endlessly.
And yet, thy breath is warm and softly tame,
When you so lovingly whisper my name.

# IV

*I* sought lust in the shadows of moonlight
On youthful instincts I could not resist
And on this errant journey did loose sight
Of stars in the wake when lovers kissed.
When, on reckless travels to distant lands
With thrills of romance that did not last,
Hard lessons were learned on hot sifting sands
That another lifestyle was to be wished.
Then came the metamorphosis of spring,
With a sobering revelation of mortality,
That I sought fulfillment true love can bring
And prayed to the high heavens for thee.
O, 'twas a magical moment of fate
To be much sooner wished for than late.

# V

*I*t was when I looked deep into your eyes,
As you touched my hand and spoke my name,
I, in epiphany, did realize
That my sad life would never be the same.
This loving desire to be one with you:
"Was my intent evolutionary?
Or, did it transpire out of the blue?
And can it be found in cupid's libr'y?"
Though this feeling I have is all so new,
Surprisingly, I feel quite beautiful
And it seems I already knew you:
"Did we transfix the supernatur'l?"
Alas, even if this passion seems surreal,
This lover's jukebox in my heart is real.

# VI

*B*ut, "Why was it me that fell prey to thee
And not the others with whom you romance?"
"And fall in love so immediately?"
"Was it my timing or or self-assurance?"
This feeling so foreign and profound to me
"How can I know if it will truly last
Or, if I am ever to be set free?"
Nothing like this have I felt in the past.
It was as if by Eros I was struck
Now wander about in a foolish daze.
"Was this my fate or a matter of luck
That upon thee desp'rate am I to gaze?"
"And what is it has my spirit so bright?"
"Could it be it was 'love at first sight'?"

# VII

*L*onging, with no courage to speak your name:
What a coward am I to fear rebuke!
How I loath this weakness and feel such shame,
I ought follow my heart in hot pursuit.
This romantic feeling is so intense
That I could love like this and live forever!
But, of course, this desire makes no sense,
Nor a wish e'en kind fates would endeavour.
O, give strength that my passions are made
known,
That I might partake of cupid's narcotic,
For further delay I cannot condone
Lest I become critically lovesick.
Yet, fears persist my love be unrequited
And with me you be not as delighted.

# VIII

My life shattered and I devastated,
I knelt on blended knee and prayed for thee,
So desperate was I to be extricated
From this loneliness and melancholy.
The heavens I entreated: "Have mercy
For I can no longer endure this life.
I beg you understand and judge me worthy
To be liberated from this strife."
Alas, it was when you whispered my name,
I realized my prayers had been heeded;
Doubtful my life will ever be the same,
For it was your love I truly needed.
One should never doubt the virtue of prayer,
Or, that one's love life is forever fair.

# IX

*N*ever to kiss your lovely face again
And feel the chill of autumn on your cheek.
"How will I ever endure this pain?"
A lovers' parting is not for the meek.
The emptiness and the disappointment
Have left me in a catatonic state,
I am unable to find contentment,
But, think only on my desperate fate.
O, how I detest such a destiny
That the fates upon me have enacted,
With a sentence of eternal misery
And my tender heart forever fracted.
O, never again will I know such love,
That fit me well as a coo to a dove.

# X

*I*t was as a matter of happenstance
That you appeared in the afterglow,
I beheld the love light of romance,
Dispersed into colours of the rainbow.
"Who can explain this phenomenon?"
"Could you be my intended mate?"
And "Is there a word in my lexicon
To define this miracle of fate?"
But soon the intense desire faded
And the passion turned to distaste,
The joy in my heart became jaded
And I began to question my haste.
Would that I could indite love for treason,
For falling in love for the wrong reason.

# XI

As the summer sun glorifies the rose,
Such was the depth of my affection
When I beheld as Michelangelo's
Your beauteous thesbian expression.
The emotion with which you spoke your lines
And the romantic tone of your voice,
I was as if framed in Valentines
And my long-imprisoned heart did rejoice.
Then as the final act concluded
With the loose ends all resolved,
I realized I was deluded
And had become with thee too involved.
Yet, so inspired to feel love in this way
And still be willing to give my heart away.

# XII

An epiphany came with a sober thought,
Despite objections to the contrary,
That is, that true, true love cannot be bought,
Though knaves who have dared are legendary.
For the many with great riches who try
To buy love without sincere affection
Face the mis'ry of their folly thereby,
And in the end ultimate rejection.
The only consideration for love
Is to be loved by someone in return,
Yet, while of money 'tis far above,
Alas, 'tis often something that we must earn.
But, unlike gold 'tis not a commodity
And if it were 'twould be an oddity.

# XIII

*I*n her culture I was "un etranger"
And though between us few words were spoken,
Surprisingly, I fell in love with her
And the silence between us was broken.
Our looks of longing and fascination
Which were e'er so innocent and discreet,
Yet, could not disguise our youthful passion,
Nor the tender sighs that were so sweet.
But, all too soon, the ship's whistle blew
And, with promises to write, we parted
As I was off to explore places anew,
Though now love-forlorned and so sad-hearted.
Love travels like the wind with no passport,
E'er greeted warmly by an open heart.

## XIV

*I*, so like the migrating butterfly,
Was thus determined to capture your heart
And savour your love before I should die
Lest I be unfulfilled there I depart.
Three lifetimes, I have waited for thee,
Midst heartfelt anguish and need,
Tossed by high winds to my destiny,
Then duped by the mimicking milkweed.
But, Hera sprang a branch on which to lite
And savour the warmth of your affection,
After enduring the perils of flight
And the hazards of my long migration.
Alas, love flies on the wings of hope,
Often by the stars in one's horoscope.

# XV

In the hurtful denouement of romance,
Love quickly melts away as "cire perdue",
For no reason other than happenstance,
If one appears to his lover untrue.
And how quickly do lovers' hearts harden,
When one of the other doth appall,
Like iron statues in a moon garden,
Upon which rain like bitter tears doth fall.
But, a lover's heart is not born of stone,
It is as delicate as porcelaine
And no matter how one attempts to atone,
Once shattered cannot be restored again.
Alas, lovers' goodbyes last forever,
For when "c'est fini!" it is over.

# XVI

There's no justice in the Court of Romance,
Which is governed by the Rules of Love,
As the parties are always biased
And the truth lies with Hora up-above.
The judgements are never astute,
With Cupid's jurisprudence in support,
Since the facts are always in dispute,
All decisions are appealed to the heart.
When sentencing at last is carried out,
On precedents for sim'lar offences,
Of gross injustice there is no doubt:
"In this court, one takes one's chances!"
But, the punishment is never amiss
And retribution is made with a kiss.

# XVII

So Innocent and yet so sensuous,
With her lovely dress she did not fret,
She was the paradigm of naturalness
So like the fashion of Marie Antoinette.
So warm and inviting were her lips,
Challenging the mightiest to resist
Transcending Into total eclipse,
Lest they be passionately kissed.
Her skin glowing midst blues and greys
And the curves of her shoulders and breasts
Enhanced the depth of her enticing gaze
And testified to her beauty blessed.
While me she undoubtedly did enthral,
She was just an ov'l tondo on the wall.

# XVIII

*W*ith lips that had recently been kissed
Passionately by her young lover,
As no ordinary man could resist,
Yet, all the while thinking of another,
She stood sensuously gazing unfocused,
More striking than can be expressed,
Holding a delicate golden crocus
Out-of-the-light as to be unnoticed.
Her open gown revealing her chest,
As she leaned 'gainst a renaissance bureau,
Chinks of sunlight captured her breast
As a maiden in a chiaroscuro.
With Loosened hair that looked so stunning,
No-one imagined she was so cunning.

# XIX

*O* how lovingly I have studied thee:
"The art world's most iconic treasure!"
By the supreme genius from Vinci,
Your importance is beyond all measure.
With an expression of enigmatic ambiguity,
Portrayed in pyramidal symmetry,
A paradigm of femininity,
Thou art as a renaissance Virgin Mary.
With your luring smile jocund by design,
You remain a Florentine mystery,
Yet, this masterpiece so truly sublime
Has made you famous throughout history.
But of your identity - "Who's to know?"
"Could you be the artist - Leonardo?"

# XX

The Champagne is no longer chilled
And the long-stemmed red roses have wilted,
The tall crystal glasses stand unfilled,
For by my love I have been jilted.
Our sweet amorations were retracted,
When deceit tossed her love like a feather,
Now my heart as a chalice lies fracted:
"How could I have been enchanted with her?"
"And what sadistic instincts were at play
That I should have been led down this path?"
As if my young heart had little to say,
But await her infliction of wrath.
Now my "Lifelove" awaits a brighter day,
When my healing tears have ebbed away.

# XXI

*I*n the lull of a zodiac spring breeze,
When I was a bud and you were in bloom,
We listened to a symphony of bees
And breathed air filled with nature's perfume.
The fauvist fairies danced with delight,
Feathering their hues well into the night,
A palette of colour for our sight,
As a rainbow in the morning light.
Your heart so affectionately tender,
As in a love story from cupid's quill,
With all its fragility and splendour,
In our own romantic garden time stood still:
As the kissing trees with lime-green leaves
Gave birth to the breeze one never sees.

# XXII

You soothed me with a foreign pastoral
And comforted me with your warm breasts,
You made it all appear so natural,
I was, with Bernice, a child blessed.
How insensitive were the hands of fate,
To claim thee in virginal wedding dress
And steal thee away sooner than late,
While I wanted lovingly to caress.
Profound grief overcame my defences
And I no longer wished to be alive
And, in this sadness, I lost my senses,
Yet, my love for you willed me to survive.
Tender memories of thee linger still,
As stars spangle the night sky, they e'er will.

# XXIII

As an unfettered bird with the love I felt,
Fin'ly so free and so liberated,
That e'en a cautious heart like mine did melt,
For dreaming of this day, I have waited.
Yet, the gifts I gave to be her fave,
To show sincerity of my intent,
As if in Irons, I became her slave
And I began to sense her discontent.
Though at times she seemed delighted,
Her feelings for me dissipated
And my love seemed unrequited,
As her sincere gratitude abated.
Alas, for me she cared not as much,
But, I remember her scent and warm touch.

# XXIV

*L*ike the zephyrs through your boughs
doth blow,
Gentle waves that ever ebb and flow,
On my heart, your love the breeze bestow
An arrow sent from Cupid's fateful bow.
How tenderly were our hearts combined,
Trapped in the mysteries of spring love,
As in a net of thee were we entwined,
Unaware of ominous clouds above.
When love comes early, the fates intervene,
Summoning all the doubts and the fears
And the hurt that may come in between,
"So regretful!" E'en after all these years.
That I knew then what I know now,
My ever weeping love, Lau Siu Lau *.

* Willow Little Willow

# XXV

*O*, such sweet and innocent affection,
As a maiden's kiss blown to a lone doe,
Ne'er did I know such sincere devotion,
Which was delicate as a feather though.
Probing and curious were her fingertips
Rippling across my skin like tide pebbles,
As her lips enticed my moon to eclipse,
Gentle and soft and lush as rose petals.
Her heart, so true and unencumbered,
Was like the refreshing zephyrs of spring
And, as a scholar, I often pondered
On how her love for me meant everything.
By sad fates we're no longer together,
But, true love like this should last forever.

# XXVI

"Acropolis: Ancient Greek Ruins"
So fraught with questions of our past,
On fallen pillars carved by humans,
Which so like their dynasties did not last.
...Caryatids on the Porch of Maidens
Elegantly supporting the temple roof,
Paid no heed to that which they were laden,
In "contrapposto" from their perch aloof...
On this walk through the ages I wonder'd:
"Will our love last beyond the end of time?"
"Is it as these ruins to be squandered?"
And "Am I a fool thinks it so sublime?"
I pray love's soul lives on in eternity,
Forgive the odd pang of uncertainty.

# XXVII

'Twas crossing San Marco's Piazza
Arm in arm against the unmarried wind,
Dodging puddles from the "acqua alta",
When our romantic love did begin.
As dark Moors their bells did chime
Ringing out the early morning hour,
Young and old to mark the passage of time,
A wing'd lion roar'd 'neath the tower.
By the piazzetta to the lagoon,
With its Doge Palace so sublime,
We felt true love under a mystic moon,
While seemingly lost in another time.
And my mask did cast a Venetian glow,
When you whispered "Io te amo".

# XXVIII

*A*pril rain had cleansed the city of light,
As we s-t-r-o-l-l-e-d along "Rue des Ecoles",
An intimate rendezvous in the night,
Young lovers mated to each other's souls.
Spring often arrives late in Paris,
To Parisians' impatient sighs,
But, unlike the canals of Venice,
It has the sweet air of paradise.
'Tis wonderful to be young and in love -
But in love "au printemps" in Paris,
With the Eiffel Tower soaring above,
Is a lover's fate for each to cherish.
"L'amour de jeunesse sans regret:
La ville lumiere" is a lover's banquet.

# XXIX

With the bouquet of ripe grapes in the air,
We biked the vineyards of Niagara,
Basking in the harvest sun without care,
Giddy from wine - then "ABRACADABRA!"
With blue skies and white clouds on the wing,
We were thunderstruck as we fell in love,
So happy were we, we began to sing,
As starlings mermurated high above.
Like an ancient mystical symbol,
Mist from "onguiaahra" came into view,
A visual indigenous signal
Proclaiming to the world our love was true.
Our forefathers knew of its magic force,
Wise were we to let nature take its course.

# XXX

It was at Club Vagabond in Leysin,
In the Vaudoise Alps of Switzerland,
Where my endless love for you did begin -
A dear mem'ry still hard to understand.
You, a rain shadow on the down-slope,
While I was a tempestuous foehn blow,
Both struggling for a modicum of hope
In radiant colours of the rainbow.
How foolish was I to ignore our love
And not realize how rare a treasure,
Now I question the heavens above
For the lives we could have shared together.
'Tis perplexing why I still lament so-
'Twas over half a century ago.

# XXXI

Walking arm-in-arm 'neath a flower moon,
While gaudy blossoms tumble in the air,
Alas with "Diana" we are so in tune -
No longer troubled and without a care.
As we sit rocking on the glide swing,
Tiny pollinators spice the silent night,
Floating delicately on the wing
And humming quietly in the moonlight.
Kissing sweet and truly in the moon glow,
Exotic tall grasses and stately trees
Attest to our joy and absence of woe,
Swaying gently in the nocturnal breeze.
'Tis lunar magic that hearts unburden,
While romancing in a moonlit garden.

# XXXII

*T*he love-struck bird pecking at the mirror
Grew excited by the image it saw,
It began to sing, as it drew nearer,
In softer tones as to express its awe.
But then it's song seemed to change its lyric,
"What was the likeness it thought it beheld?"
"Was it a mate or a feathered spirit?
Or, an enemy it ought have repelled?"
A mystery in ornithology,
It soon became a constant obsession
And a study in erotology,
Whatever the cespitose attraction.
Yet, our tunes so mirror those of "love birds"
Our love a joyful birdsong beyond words.

# XXXIII

So enraptured with the Caravaggio,
She stood transposed by his great masterpiece,
As her tears like a spring rindle did flow,
Her tender heart stripped of restful peace.
So profound the depth of her sorrow therein,
She was as one of the loving grieved,
Thus moved by the sad death of the Virgin,
The scene depicted she truly believed
...Virgin Mary clad in a robe of red
Surrounded by apostles in woeful grief,
She lies reclined with lolling head,
While Mary Magdeline mourns in disbelief...
'Tis a gift to feel vicariously,
A true lover's palette obviously.

# XXXIV

"Could we love were we to live forever?"
"Would romantic feelings be as intense?"
"Would the hearts of lovers be as tender?"
"Would loving anyone at all make sense?"
Alas time would not be as precious
Nor as fleeting as the wandering moon,
Nor lovers' entreaties compendious,
Nor could a love affair be o'r too soon.
"Does ephemeral time fan lovers hearts
Knowing the flames will not last forever,
Stoking the fire impassioned love imparts
That welds their adoring hearts together?
And, does this love extend beyond time?"
This would be "unquestionably" sublime.

# XXXV

Weeping teary words into breaking night,
With a fixed look of resignation
And with not an alternative in sight,
Knew leaving was the only solution.
With no semblances of love to reprise,
The hurt caused by his infidelity,
His philandering and insufferable lies
Fractured their amorous reality.
With no progeny and little intent,
Which his disarming charm could not disguise,
In stead, she gave birth to resentment
And only her cheeks her tears did baptize.
'Tis love unrequited breeds discontent:
To love unloved is a lover's lament.

# XXXVI

*L*ike kiting through space on a spider's web,
As if migrating to some foreign land,
'Neath the sun, the moon and stars overhead-
'Tis a voyage I don't quite understand.
"To where?" and "How far?" Tis up to the wind,
Landing in the ocean or on the shore,
So like penance for those who've sinned,
Or ultimate reward to those due more.
And on this journey destiny prevails,
With no assurance of a kindly fate
And heartache if the adventure fails:
"O, the chances one takes to find a mate!"
An arduous quest not for the meek,
But the courageous who love do seek.

# XXXVII

The old willow waved its final goodbyes
Before the devil wind hacked it in two,
And all around one could hear its sighs-
So like the parting between me and you.
It now lies divided and in a heap,
Its wounds fresh and unfaded,
Its sagging branches fast asleep,
With their leaves shrinking and jaded.
The merciless wind gives no time to mourn,
Sweeping over its victims in glee-
So like the anger and burning scorn
Those tempests between you and me.
Alas, to relate so vicariously
To the death of a weeping willow tree.

# XXXVIII

The poet's love sonnets were not yet spun
Dormant, like the seeds of desert flora
'Neath the sand and the blazing sun
Awaiting the damp dawn of Aurora.
Romance reinvigorated the poet,
Torrential rain the quiescent seeds
And the joy in the verses did show it,
Like festive garlands of kissed daisy beads.
Love inspires like rain to wilderness
Giving life to all struggling to survive,
A desert for a prophet's eyes to rest
And an overwrought heart to revive.
One must never shy from love's paradox,
There are places where trees grow out of rocks.

# XXXIX

A rainbow in the mist of summer's light,
Colouring landscapes in my view so gay
And starlight in the heart of winter's night,
Guiding me along my troublesome way,
A child of mother nature she was made,
In harmony with body and spirit
And closer to me than colour to jade,
As the fates deemed her love I did merit.
And when the rich colours began to fade
And the glittering light began to dim,
Romantic love the paradigm she'd made,
As the heroine in a cupid's hymn.
In matters of the heart, 'tis just to say:
That of lovers all, she was "A Per Se!"

# XL

*I* fantasized that my lover had gone
Like Asteria faded into night,
In silence long before the break of dawn
Forever taken from my wonted sight.
And I so desperate began to weep,
Believing that my heart was shattered,
And the hurt felt was so profoundly deep
That I thought my life no longer mattered.
Then I heard a melody at my ear-
A lyric from a romantic love song;
'Twas my love urging me to come near,
Which is by my nature where I belong.
Gratefully, dreams are not reality,
So like readings from a Greek deity...

# XLI

With our lovelock set on the Bridge of Love
Engraved with "N" and "R", we tossed the keys
Then blew a kiss to a turtle dove,
As it dove in the warm Serbian breeze.
Romantic sweethearts then were you and I,
As you were off to a war like no other,
And on our bridge we said our sad goodbye
Not knowing if it would be forever.
In Corfu, love drew you to another,
Sadly, our affair was terminated -
A matter from which I have yet to recover,
As my love for you has ne'er abated.
While our lock on our bridge has long since
gone,
Your lock on my aging heart is e'er strong.

N - Nada R – Relja

# XLII

The sign read: "Want Kindness - Spare Change -
God Bless".
They were sprawled on crushed cardboard in the
park,
Both with no destination and homeless
"Smokin'" and "cuddlin'" and "waitin'" for dark.
They met at a soup kitchen in the Bow'ry
"It was a crazy, magical moment"
She said, "He just overpowered me
And saved me from my ongoing torment."
The abuse, the sickness and the drugs,
One cannot know the hardships they have seen,
He protects her from the perverts and the thugs
And makes her feel as if she were a Queen.
She swears they are forever a couple-
Off to make love in the subway tunnel.

# XLIII

*A* high brideprice paid for his daughter's hand,
Though he had not requested her consent,
In support of which her suitor did stand
Given the fortune that he had spent.
But alas, his love was unrequited,
As she longed to be with another,
He felt he had been deceived and spited
And tossed as if he were a dove's feather.
Trying to elope she was arrested
And savagely killed by friends and family,
By all villagers she was detested,
As if they had all lost their sanity.
Tragic love flies on the wings of the raven,
Killed for "honor" lovers with no haven.

# XLIV

*A* young "ill-starred" Venetian beauty
Of love for a Moor General did sing.
Cursed by her father for shirking duty,
Defended her husband before the King.
But, the loss of a gifted handkerchief,
In the hands of one meant to deceive,
Gave rise to a sinister plot of mischief
And claims of infidelity did weave.
Strangling her on grounds of adultery,
How tragic the Moor's fate to discover
That villainous clues to the contrary,
She was an honest and faithful lover.
Love's passion and jealousy breed contempt,
Violent reactions are not exempt.

# XLV

*I*n the monotony of a long wait,
I close my eyes and utter a bored sigh,
I recall the time of year and the date,
As I lament life quickly passing by.
These moments in lifetime so desolate:
"Will my legacy ever be complete?"
"Will I have even reached a mature state
And not have given in to self-defeat?"
"Will I give a wink at Dame Fickle Fate
As to say the mighty odds have been beat?
Or will I give way to regretful hate
And collapse in sheer anguish at her feet?"
Then enters my love and as I embrace her
Fates and fleeting time no longer matter.

# XLVI

*I*n love, I thrice cried out your Persian name
And without fear rushed to ring thrice the gong,
'Twas your beauty and my passion to blame,
Three riddles to wed and death if I'm wrong.
"What is born each night and dies each dawn?"
"Hope!"
"What flickers red and warm like a flame?"
"Blood!"
"What is the ice that makes you burn?"
"Turandot!"
I've won your hand and muted the axe's thud.
Consoling, I gave a riddle to thee:
"Discover my name before next sunrise
And from this marriage I will set thee free!"
Then trusting my love gave up my disguise.
With a kiss, hate your heart did rise above
And when asked my name you shouted "'Tis
Love!"

# XLVII

*W*e marvelled at mother of pearl clouds,
Sought after treasures and waded through
streams,
Hugged tightly as the night enshrouds
And kissed so passionately in my dreams.
How often I've thought of you in my life,
Imagining how and when we would meet,
That you would acquiesce to be my wife
And with love make my lonely life complete.
But, you're the hidden star in the night's sky
As different as colors of the season,
Of your identity, I wonder why
It changes often and without reason.
I pray the fates destine our hearts to greet
And, as in my dreams, you will be as sweet.

# XLVIII

"*How* will I know if you are my lovemate?"
How will I know if I should take a chance?"
"How will I know if it is my true fate?"
"How will I know if it is fake romance?"
And "Should I trust the feelings of my heart?"
Or "Should I defer only to reason?"
"Should I the wisdom of others impart?"
Or "Should I acquiesce to the season?"
And "If there is a modicum of doubt
Undermining my true feelings of love",
Or "If I fear I know not what I'm about,
Then should I knee and pray to God above?"
No matter the outcome of romance,
There is always an element of chance.

# XLIX

We're born into a devine mystery,
Our loving hearts a miracle of life,
An enigma pondered throughout hist'ry
And not without a modicum of strife.
"Where did we come from?" "Where are we
going?"
Metaphysical questions do abound,
With philosophers not truly knowing
And ontological theories all-round.
But of my love there is no conundrum,
As it is one thing of which I am sure,
That for thee my heart did rightly succumb
And miracle or not, it will endure.
On this my adoration will ever show,
For love's the only thing I truly know.

# L

*A*n unfledged scholar was driven off course
By the wayward winds of his libido,
His uncharted passion's ill-fated curse
And perils of his Inflated ego.
Squandering his tuition on "Tom's pay"
And rash affairs that were so indiscreet,
Unaware of the dangers and foul play,
Naive was he of the ways of the street.
Then, when a jealous lover took offence
And in a fit of anger pulled a gun,
While hopelessly pleading his innocence,
He lost sight forever of the teary sun.
And all for brief moments of shameful bliss,
While lost in a lane lover's unholy kiss.

# LI

"What season is this now?" "I do not know!'
So fragile was he and she in despair,
Seeing the silver sky and swhirling snow,
As she gently combed his thinning white hair.
He, sitting sedated and beseeming,
And she, so dedicated and tender,
Tried to hide the anguish she was feeling
While he struggled in vain to remember.
Unaware of their lifelong love affair
And e'er in anticipation waiting,
As he muttered what seemed like a prayer,
For a quick, lovely death masquerading.
Depleting quickly his life-timer sand,
He slowly reach out with his trembling hand.

# LII

*I*n the denouement of a fauvist dream,
As though I was looking through a sallett,
I marvelled at the colours that I'd seen
So like those on an artist's palette.
Some colours were like friends of the others
Some like neighbours, sisters and brothers
Those that were attracted were their lovers
And some like rainbows were babes and
mothers.
But a single colour stood high above,
As it gave meaning to life and the arts,
It was the brilliant colour of love -
The one that is painted on our hearts.
While objects of the eye will ever jade
The colour of our love will never fade.

# LIII

*T*heir families in the midst of feuding hate
A metaphor of sin and saints did greet
Young Veronesi lovers doomed by fate
Lost in an unnamed kiss tender and sweet.
A hasty, secret marriage concluded
And their holy union consummated
With a friar's hope for peace eluded
Their religion of love's still debated
For in a plot meant her own death to feign
Deeming his love poisoned he too did take
Welcomed his dagger to relieve her pain
When she awoke to realize his mistake.
Though I'll-starred was their destiny
Their love's legend lives in eternity.

# LIV

Our merry carousel waltz has ended
The flying horses no longer go 'roun'
The organ music has long ago faded
For our circus has already left town.
Perhaps I was masquerading
Pretending to be someone I am not
And with commitment always evading
So like the harlequin ...with love forgot.
Now it all seems like such a sideshow
And I don't know how or what to feel
Of those moments of joy and scenes of woe
Like the highs and lows of a Ferris wheel.
Sound as a striker bell true love can be
When not, melts away like cotton candy.

# LV

In the dark depression of a heartbreak
I am broken with no desire to live
Her precious love which the ill fates did take
Is a loss I'm unable to survive.
'Twas Thanatos came to reap with his sword
As we laid at peace in our nuptial bed
The best wishes for "long life" all ignored
When Atropos severed her young life's thread.
Resting still beside me as if asleep
I whispered the coming of our new dawn
And of the what-to-do's that would not keep
But then I realized that she was gone.
Weeping, I gave her one final caress
Then buried her in her white wedding dress.

# LVI

*P*osing so like a statue in a niche
Enshrouded in a marblesque cloak
Enchantedly, your stare did me bewitch
As burning ambergris bathed you in smoke.
Like a magical symphony in white,
So inviting I did not feel remiss
When, like a thief in the stillness of night,
Invaded your holy purge to steal a kiss.
Tasting your warm lips as I met your eyes
I was possesed by aphrodesia
Though aromata continued to rise
Alas, I was en route to Amoresia.
'Twas like living a lovers' fairytale
All from the regurgence of a whale.

# LVII

*N*ear Lake Gokul under a new blood moon
His bamboo flute soothed all into trance
So handsome was he the maids did swoon
And smitten Gopis around him would dance.
With aura of blue, he met their desires
Until a Gopi whose beauty was art
Quench'd those mischievous burning fires
As she danced and captured his heart.
Though some would say it is just a fable
This profound love became their destiny
And their names holy and inseparable
Were sung with a pure blissful melody.
The milkmaid and flautist ever entwined
Soulmates Raghu and her Krishna devine.

# LVIII

"Ex chrysalis" spurts a dash of colour
The elongated neck of a lover
Created with disdain and disorder
Sensuous nudes cherished the world over.
Defying any classification
And indifferent to avant garde art
Never a slave to his reputation
He painted with an ever valiant heart.
But for him tragedy was no stranger
Struggling with his illness and addiction
There were many lives he put in danger
And informed an early death's prediction.
Dying with his pregnant love by his side
Heartbroken she committed suicide.

# LIX

*T*rapped in a tempestuous love affair
Filled with such tragic temptation
And not being consciously aware
Of his evolving emasculation,
A Roman general of diminished pride
Became a slave to her Egyptian charms
And when hearing of her feined suicide
Wounded himself and died in her arms.
The Queen so heartbroken and desperate,
Then bowed to the royalty of an asp
And from its venom accepted her fate
Crying out his name in her final gasp.
Though manipulated to his last breath,
He redeemed himself by his "noble" death.

# LX

*I*n my hidden sadness and troubled mind
I became aware our love could not last
Though your heart for me was never unkind
Gone were the feelings I had in the past.
Was it fear that life was passing me by
That my future was out of my control
Or was I just searching to satisfy
The restlessness I felt in my soul.
Yet, as tender thoughts of you persist
A deep voice within me ponders whether
The warm affections we shared still exist
Though we are no longer together.
For in strictest confidence, between we two,
In quiet darkness, I still dance with you!

# LXI

Migrating to you on a cool spring night
So desirous of your passionate love
And weary from a searching lover's flight
Guided by the lonely stars above.
Lost in an embrace far away from shore
Unaware was I of the current's flow
The swift rapids turbulence and roar
Of the tragedy that awaited me below.
Falling through mist and unable to fly
As if caught in a nightmarish trap
Fearful that I was about to die
Instinctively, my wings began to flap.
Though weak, I flew back o'er the thun'dring falls
Escaping libido's tragic love calls.

# LXII

*T*here were no "chinks of light" in the darkness
"Riding the wave" and what love was tough
With my vanishing youth in such distress
Of this worthless life, I had had enough.
Then on a mean dateless night you appear
Your empathic voice purged my solitude
And when you said "You do not belong here!"
My bloodied knees buckled in gratitude.
"What was it made you put your trust in me?"
"Was it my looks or something that I said?"
For your true kindness changed my destiny
And without it I know I would be dead.
O how I long to be with my strangel
Whom I know as my guardian angel.

# LXIII

*H*er eyes like black holes in the universe
Into which my life's energy did flow
A projected astral sorceress curse
Filling my heart with suffering and woe.
A force so profound it captured my sight
And warped the space-time fabric of my soul
And reshaped with empyrean delight
Mind, life and transcendental passions whole.
Then like a comet's death dive to the sun
Her mystic love lost its radiant glow
As legend Icarus's flight undone
Or like "white dwarfs" a billion years ago.
Yet, when I gaze into the sky at night,
Zeus knows I'll love her longer than starlight.

Lightning Source UK Ltd.
Milton Keynes UK
UKHW022042200120
357311UK00008B/303

9 780228 825937